# IN THE GATHERING OF SILENCE

# In the
# Gathering of Silence

poems by
## Levi Romero

West End Press

Some of these poems have previously appeared in the following publications: *THE magazine, Crosswinds, Blue Mesa Review, Arellano, The River Styx, Blanco Movil* (Mexico), and *Saludos!*

This project is supported in part by a grant from the National Endowment for the Arts, a federal agency.

First edition, August 1996
ISBN 0-931122-84-8

Front cover drawing by Levi Romero
Back cover photograph of the author by Michael Reed
Cover design and book design by Michael Reed
Typography by Prototype, Albuquerque, NM

Distributed by the University of New Mexico Press

West End Press • P.O. Box 27334 • Albuquerque, New Mexico 87125

para Elias y Carolina
y lo que sobrevive
trayendo vida y amor

I was dumb with silence
I held my peace,
even from good:
and my sorrow
was stirred.
My heart was hot
within me,
while I was musing
the fire burned:
then spake I
with my tongue

Psalm 39

Alain Romeo
1926

# CONTENTS

## I. A Good Trampe is Hard to Find

## II. Easynights and a Pack of Frajos

## III. Of Dust and Bone

Se ha usado el lenguaje del norte de Nuevo Mexico.

# I.
# A Good Trampe is Hard to Find

## Tres Copas de Chanate
## Black and Sweet

órale ese
saludes de south fourth
spicy street overflowing with
creamy joy and scornful sorrow
resembling a faded watercolor painting
rotting under the sun
growing tangled 'neath the billboard
bosom sighs of a new frontier

I have felt you waking up sweating
to the sounds of 3 a.m. trains
rolling in on greasy tracks
spreading across your innocence
like melting butter on a hot tortilla

your gold toothed mouth of prominence
has gone silent under the weight
of rusted steel and faded brick
where cash registers once sang
like Christmas chimes

on your black heeled streets
bleed tattooed backs in blue ink
penance for your soul
proud puro Barelas 13

your chapped dusty sidewalks
kissing the calloused souls
of homeless saints
rising out of trash bins
in the red eyed dawn
are fed by the black vein freeways
dripping diseased America
into your dirt alley dreams

your complaints become rheumatoid groans
of aching feet sliding across linoleum
floors towards clock radios weeping
Mexican ballads into the trumpet gold
haze of memories too strong to stick
or sink into the Río Grande mud
me llamo Manuel Leyba
but they call me manual labor

behind the soot screen windows
and padlocked doors of the Redball Cafe
sit chrome and metalflake countertops
frozen in the chewy silence
of a Catholic Sunday ringing sad
a billion more still yearn
to be served

pickup trucks once danced into
the Royal Fork restaurant parking lot
from Gallup and Farmington
slipping through the honeydew
sweetness of ripening September

oh, earth goddess
of asphalt and grime
let me hear your hearty laugh
flapping heavy like El Cambio's
storefront window ads
that fill my salty visions
with sweet roll promises
crumbling onto the dry
tongue of my worn-out shoes

## Gone

my father
    isn't
        dead

he's
    just
        gone

gone as the
    wet nose cows
        he used
            to keep

gone as the
    old trucks
        that he
            drove

gone as the
    driving rain
        pouring into
            the scars

of the eroding
    now gone
    road

there was a
    tiny pricked hole
        near his right
            ear lobe

I never asked
    where or
        how he
            got it

and he would
    sing songs
        as he drove

fragments of songs
    songs he must've
        sung

when he
    was in
        the war

thinking of his
        faraway
            gone
                mother

his
    father's
        donkeys

and
    his
        querida

his querida

    my mother

I found an
    old suitcase
        in granma's
            attic

belonging to my father
            and it was
                full of
                    letters

letters
    from my
        mother

sealed with
    a lipstick
        kiss

and a
    picture

a picture of
    a beautiful
        blonde girl

a girl from
    across the
        sea

the one who must've
                kept him
                        going

through
        all the
                gone

of
        all the
                gone

all
        the
                gone

all
        the
                gone

all
        the
                gone

# Wheels

how can I tell you
baby, oh honey, you'll
never know the ride
the ride of a lowered chevy
slithering through the
blue dotted night along
Riverside Drive Española

poetry rides the wings
of a '59 Impala
yes, it does
and it points
chrome antennae towards

'Burque stations rocking
oldies Van Morrison
brown eyed girls
Creedence and a
bad moon rising
over Chimayo

and I guess
it also rides
on muddy Subarus
tuned into new-age radio
on the frigid road
to Taos on weekend
ski trips

yes, baby
you and I are two
kinds of wheels
on the same road

listen, listen
to the lonesome humming
of the tracks we leave
behind

# Proud Side of Town

they are well-
read

and it almost makes
me feel
naive

but I don't

shadows cut
a forty five
degree

against a peeling
wall

I reach for
the door to
step

into the kind
of place

they would never
enter

I am well-
lived

## Los Heroes

los watchávamos
cuando        pasaban
echando jumito azul
en sus ranflas aplanadas
como ranas
de ojelata

eran en los días
de los heroes

cuando había heroes
turriqueando en
lengua mocha
y riza torcida

Q-volé

ahora nomás        pasan
los recuerdos
uno tras del otro
y mi corazón
baila

bendición

bendición es
estar contento

Señor gracias por . . .

gracias por
todo

## La Huera Negra


gray skies weeping
over Negro in the hospital bed
big black volcano exploding
forty years of vida dura loca
heartache attack erupting 2 o'clock morning
at Our Lady of Assumption Rectory
Padre Luis tip toe frantic
screeches Lomas Boulevard awake

                    a la chingada Negro!
                        ¿Qué paso?

everything comes crashing
splitting our lives
with the swiftness of an axe blade
on a Costilla winter's grunt
hachasos retumbando cold steel awakening
for Las Vegas to Los Chavez
our sadness becomes a nervous laugh

embracing belly of misfortune
turns afternoon solidarity
the color of a cold tile floor
but we lay our faith across the path
of a long black train disappearing
into the sleepless night
as we pace hallways from Panama to Portugal
with our hard faces melting like wax
wondering if you're gonna come back to life

images of friends forgotten
and foes forgiven
develop under your eyelids
and fall back into
your box of color slides
stored away now
in La Ruca's lilac blossom springs
of your juventud

tonight's candle flames
burning dark light sorrow
and the Boys Club llorona

clasping our hand down
Mountain Road memory
keep vigil with a
thousand green-eyed saints
baring a toothless winner's grin

we await your triumphant
return into crazy vida
and we're gonna eat frijoles and tortillas
at Tomas's

es
    todo
        carnal

           es
    todo
  por
hoy

es
    todo
      por
        siempre

nos tenemos que poner truchas

con la huera negra

la Sweet Sebastian
  de los campos

porque nos trae ganas

y como dice primo Bill

"si me trae ganas,
que no las aguante"

    -pepinos total-

## Village Duck

I picked up Gonito
as I was passing through town one day
I inquired about several people
but all he would say was
"quack, quack"

¿Gonito, que le has hecho, como está todo?
"quack, quack, quack"
¿qué razón me das de tal y tal?
"quack, quack"

just a bit down the road
he noisily gestured that he wanted off
so I pulled over to let him out

bueno, Gonito, ay te miro
he just answered back
in a flurry of duck noises
"quack, quack, quack, quack"

as I drove away
I looked in the rear view mirror
and saw him squatting down the road
teasing the dogs of the village
"quack, quack, quack"

I guess he was just being
a duck that day

# You greet me

with the casual tap
of a deep Mexico memory
and a hug slow 'n' hot
as a torch song dance

we meet here on midnight's
naked road as a mystery unraveled
    guided by the flat and empty rise
    of a discernible yearning
    and the backroad's dark invitation

yet, we know
by the shadows we keep
we are strangers to each other

the fractions of time
adding up to this moment
keep to themselves
what we reach for in touching
    we are apparitions of our ghostly remains
    consumed by the stumble and catch
    of our invisible selves

    on this plane
    where the abstract melds into the obscure
we slip and slide in the rising pulse
of what seems so at once
hauntingly profound and fatally pure

having gained only the loss
of a risk denied and reduced
by the measured reflection
of the distance untraveled
    we are where we stand
    like the night now
    dark eyed and wanting

# On Mornings Like These

On mornings like
these
when dawn is still
sleeping fetal prone
it is
on mornings like
these
when the whole world
echoes in the sound
of nothing
when my mind
is devoured by thoughts
of wild ponies
on mornings like
these
when one hundred miles
is an eternity's length away
from the one who yearns
for me
on mornings like
these
I'll wake knowing
I'm the only one
to keep me company
it is
on mornings like
these
when I reach into
the same pocket twice
for a pen to write with
on mornings like
these

# It Goes On In That Way

I remember that day on FM Hill

>we were just hanging out drinking beer
>there was nothing really special about that day
>other than they don't happen like that anymore

>there were a few of us
>'though I can't recall exactly who, but Mague

I remember him

>flat-topped white-haired Korean war veteran
>with faded tattoos and a crazy laugh
>and he was crouching low to the ground

>he took a good hit from some homegrown
>raised his head towards the sky
>and blew the smoke into his beer can
>and then took a good swallow

I remember that

>because I thought that maybe it was
>some special magic trick going towards infinity
>'cause I knew he'd come down a long road
>and carried with him secrets
>of an unspoken trade

I remember him today

>beyond the skyline of this city
>the noise of crows and the freeway traffic
>and I tip my can in remembrance

>to the gray sky
>and the black volcanoes
>and to Mague

>it goes on
>in that way

remembering, remembering

>it goes on in that way
>it goes on in that way

# II.
# Easynights and a Pack of Frajos

# Easynights and a Pack of Frajos

Rosendo used to ride the buses
scoring phone numbers from rucas
he'd meet at the parque or
along Central's bus stops and diners

    three to five numbers a day, homes
    he'd say, by the end of the week
    I know I'll get lucky with
    at least one, 'ey

    maybe she'll have her own canton
    and I'll drop by with a bottle of wine
    and some good herb
    y vamonos recio, carnal

and he'd laugh, tilting his head back
taking a long drag from a Camel regular
and then he'd look at me
and laugh again, saying

    iii, éste vato!
    sometimes I just don't know
    about you, bro.

one night I was shooting pool down at Jack's
when the bartender yelled out
that there was a phone call
for someone whose name sounded like mine
and I was real surprised
that it was for me, you know

well, it was this fine babe from the Westside
that I'd met a few weeks before
she said that my roommate
had told her I'd be there
she said she'd been wondering
what I'd been doing
and how come I hadn't called

she wanted me to go over
so I said yeah, o.k.
I'll be there in a while
but I want to shoot a couple more games

not that I was really interested
in pool anymore
but, hey I couldn't let on
like I didn't ever get
those kinda calls, you know

not like those vatos at Tito's
with tattoos and dead-aim stares did
leaning back against the wall
flirting with some ruca over the phone
laughing and teasing while the jukebox
plays Sam Cooke and me sitting there
watching and wondering where I
went wrong going right

I asked her if there's anything
she wants me to bring over
some wine, maybe
and she says, yeah
that sounds good
and could you bring some cigarettes too

so there I am
going down the street
being all truchas for the jura
'cause I didn't want nothin'
to ruin this movida, you know

well, I pulled into the Casa Grande
and asked for a bottle of Easynights
and a pack of frajos
and I sat looking through the drive-up window
at the naked pinup girls on the wall

and I started thinking of home
so far away
and how oftentimes
I had nowhere to go
wishing I knew some nice girl
I could drop by to visit
and watch a mono with
or just to sit and talk to

it was a rainy night
a beautiful rainy night
and the streets were all black and wet

neon lights reflecting off of everything
and running down the street
in streams of color

and I thought of Rosendo
and how he was going to laugh
and I knew he was going to want
to know everything

    órale, serio?
    chale, you're jiving, homes

    no, serio
    her name's Carmela

    serio, homes?

    yeah!

    no?

    yeah, de veras!

    iii, éste vato!

then I looked in the mirror
and I started laughing

    sometimes I just don't know
    about you, bro.

## Santero

qué a gusto
qué a gusto te miras, Pate
quitado de penas
sentando resolaneando
echándote un Vel'

pero tu sonrisa aprietada
y ojos brillando
son testigos que entera
la vida de cabeza comienza
y se acaba en pedazos
sobre los pies

con los años nos
parecemos bultos doblados
asistiendo lumbres
con cuipas y cáscaras
que al fin de ceniza a ceniza
han de volver

ay, compadre,
nos corre la sangre negra
venas goteando gotas de vino
y estas lágrimas pegajosas
como trementina sobre mi cara
que no se me quieren secar

entre más lindo el arbolito
más presto cae
y aquellos hachasos helados
quebrando por las cañaditas
en un diciembre

me tuvieron en recuerdo
de que el mismo resuello
que nos da vida
también es el cual
nos la puede quitar

inspiración por la obra
de Edward Gonzales
"Patroncinio Barela"

22

# alibi

when the cop pulled up
I wondered how we were gonna explain all this
'cause when you're doing something
it's not too hard to lie,
but when you're doing nothing
well, what can you say

> "we're just sitting here officer,
> just talking, and he's writing poetry"

I mean, how's that really gonna sound
to a guy who means business
and carries a gun

## One Yesterday at a Time

blind curve thoughts
and a small offering for you
from the sandy stone slopes
of the Sandias' east side
engaged in meditative
backseat observance
sipping clear Santa Fe Blush
in one hundred-degree traffic jam weather
    where the poetics of August rise
    from roadside alfalfa stems
    swaying saintlike to hot mother rhythm

stretching on through napping Carnuel's
dog tongue panting afternoon
    sleepy town road weaving
    like a rattlesnake through the brush
past mother and kids pouring gas
into family sedan
and sun-licked men with Virgen Guadalupanas
tattooed on their backs laying felt
on the rooftop sizzling sweat

above the pestering chicharra chorus 'n' rhyme
horns blare impatience
while silent Our Fathers
rise from behind the clouded horizon
as we make our way past
crushed metal and broken glass
steaming out've the asphalt heat

post-adolescent anxiousness
blowing hot breeze cynicism
    in and out
of the fast turn towards
mining town curios
rain puddle blessings
and windshield fantasies
polished smooth to the feel
of a tiger's eye

sinking deep into hymn book philosophy
again 'n' again rising
to knee bent heights
with a heavy load of unconscious act
pouring over the side rails
    and yes we shall overcome
        un día a la vez
          Dios mio
        un día a la vez

# The Silence Always

his gaze wandered out through the screen door
into the back yard
out to a small patch of tomatoes and squash

there in the silence of the afternoon
like everything else of late
he thought
this silence too was deceiving

he heard the slight hush of a breeze
sweeping a hanging vine
across the doorstep
and noticed the refrigerator's slow hum
as it came and went

in the overgrowth of
unkept bushes and dead limb fruit trees
he could spot the insects flicking
across the yard
lately the notion of leaving
had come to him again

had it not been almost three years ago
on an afternoon like this
when he stood hitchhiking
out of that small town
at the southern edge of Colorado

she had enticed him with the thought
of coming out here and spending time
a quick trip and the possibility
of love flourishing like the wild grass
after the soft rains that came
each afternoon that summer

but that season was over
and so too he thought
were the wonderful lovemaking afternoons
and long evening walks along the creek

so when she said
you seem so far away
like the clouds in the distance

that keep promising rain
he didn't quite catch it
his mind was already long over the fence
and down the road beyond
these last few years

he appeared to accept this philosophically
but the silence betrayed him
the silence always
the silence
louder than words

# Gavilan

en memoria de un gavilan:
Rudy "Sunny" Sanchez

aquí estoy sentado
en una silleta coja y desplumada
recordando aquellas amanecidas
cuando nos fuimos grandes y altos

en aquel tiempo que nos encontrabanos
sin pena ninguna
cuando la vida pa' nosotros
apenas comienzaba y la tarea
era larga y llena de curiosidades

entretenidos siempre con
aquel oficio maldito
un traguito para celebrar
la vida
y otro para disponer
la muerte

ayer bajo las sombras
de los gavilanes que vuelavan
con sus alas estiradas
como crucitas negras
en contra del sol
pense en ti
tú que también fuites
gavilan pollero

con una locura verdadera
y aquella travesura sin fin
hoy como ayer
tus chistes relumbrosos
illuminando estas madrugadas solitarias
que a veces nos encuentran medios norteados
y con las alas caidas

tal como esos polleros
tirando el ojo por el cerrito de La Cuerda
así también seguiremos rodeando, carnal
carnal de mano
y de palabra
amistad que nació
en aquel amanecer eterno

y si no nos topamos
en esta vuelta
pues entonces, compa
pueda que en la otra

# Hearts and Arrows

in memoriam: Levi Sandoval

hearts and arrows
are engraved with lovers' names
on the old doors
of the mission school

it is almost noontime
and nostalgia gleams
with the dull brilliance
of a chrome airplane
on the rusty hood
of a '56 Chevy

dog-worn trails
cut across my memory
like the jagged edges
of broken wine bottles
that once lay snarling
at my feet

the high-pitched roofs
seem to push and turn
under the stillness
of the Sangre de Cristos
where remnants from
decades past lie caked
in dust-dead attics
under hot tin

as the crackling heat
falls through the trees
and rolls across
the sweet apricot ground

a screen door bangs
'neath a porch
where a woman with a broom
sways to the broken rhythm
of a forgotten song
while chickens peck through
the casual silence of a
tomorrow's promise already
come and gone

daydreams of walking barefoot
on the soft grass
down by the river
where dragonflies buzzed all day
have now decayed
like fallen cottonwoods
along the gnarled paths
of the Río Embudo

where free-form poetry
mixed with cheap beer
on warm nights by the riverbanks
and stories of lowered '49 Fleetlines
with flamejobs and spinners
were cast into the dark wind

all that remains
are ash-cold memories
of a flaming fire

finally quenched
     with
          tears

# Ombligonas

it is fifteen minutes
　from the Mexican border
　　but the language of love
　　　crosses quicker than that

strangers shaded 'neath the hot
　by orange trees
　　and cool conversation

the far is entwined
　with the near
　　and we laugh
　　　in our longing

our tongues hushed
　by the drop
　　of an orange

it is an equalled gravity
　and we are brought down
　　by that moment so born

when our handshake in parting
　strengthens the umbilical twist
　　in this life ever passing

# Something About My Father

something he said to me
that I recalled today

it was not in the shape of his words
or in the language that he used

for he had mastered those well

but rather it was in the way
the tears glazed his eyes
and did not leave the surface
of the pupil

and there at the end

I had learned somehow
to read that look
and had come to realize then
that it had not always been
from a night of too much drinking

that look
hard and tarnished like old silver

my father
beautiful man

who had mastered his tears
there at the end

where words had no value
or a warranty that came

with promises unkept

# Jazzmin

white boys were blowing
cool jazz in Aspen

candle lit marble top
tables and gin and tonics
crisp as the night air

the brass trombone
sunk notes
and golden tanned legs
dangled from stools

white skirts
Independence Pass

diggin' dew-dropped
        be-bop
                hey!

# I Miss You Tonight

this night in the deep breath
of solitude
I wake
with my hand cupped and shaped
to hold your breast

but my arms empty of embrace
are like late October's branches
reaching out to catch
the falling leaves
     only to clutch the emptiness of air

and yet those words
have not come to me
    the
        I DO
          I WILL

so it is
    that I am still afraid
    to release that long barren season
    in my life

yielding now at thirty years of age
a season finally bearing fruit

and you
    sweet love
these last few months
having bloomed and blossomed
    to meet the harvest
    of my youth

in my untrodden path
    there are stones yet
    to be cleared
and so it will be

when twilight undrapes
the heavy folds of this sorrow
loomed over with the weight
    of a warm comfort
        turned cold

oh, it will come
that day
     your love in mine

though the moon turns
on a slow leaf tonight
this night
     contained bent and heavy
         at the limb

# III.
# Of Dust and Bone

## Lindy's

we sit in the gathering
of silence
    Picasso-faced men
    hunched along the counter
    like birds on a line

the guilt of innocence rising
for the lack of
    a quarter uncompromised
    over a cup of coffee

numbcast reflections on the pie shelf
startle us not
    by what became
    but by what could have

"give me your poems" she said
"out of your closet"
    failing to notice his face
    wore all his belongings

today the bleeding sun
with its red core hollow
    pick-pockets the soul
    takes a handful of nothing

# Of Dust and Bone

do I hear
'mano Anastacio's
muddy mystic drawl

coming over brain waves
fuzzy as AM radio
nights        long time ago

when we slept outdoors
in the humming
summer
drinking Cokes and Dr Peppers
eating Dorito chips and

strumming broom guitars
to Band On The Run
with the transistor radios
tuned in to
X-ROCK 80 or OKLAHOMA

seventh grade crushes
and teasing howls
in the mooing cow dusk
and hopping toad yards
lit in golden orange

adobe dust
on my brow
and burning, yearning,
learning, love exploding
from my heart

like bottle rockets
on the starry spangled
Fourth of July

where are you lain
little dipper dreamers
who once stirred
under granma's homemade
blankets in the dewy breath
of early morn

when grandfathers
with shovels slung
across their shoulders
headed for the ditchbanks
to open up their
gates

oh, July apple
suckling summer with the
sweet and bitter taste
of wisdom's tears trickling
down your pink mountain
slopes

I see you
I feel you
I hear you
dying
to be born again

oh, fathers' graves
with splintered crosses
swaying skyline bare
under a November
moon

whose resurrection burneth
through the flaming hearts
of your displaced
sons

and from snowflake
whiskered men
mumbling broken mouthed
forgotten ancient prayer
of dust and bone

in the plaza
where rainbow haloed angels
crowned with a wreath
of wild country flowers
blow their groggy
horns

I hear you
yes, I hear you 'mano Anastacio

I hear you cawing
like a lone crow
in the pines

# Three Chord Riff

Juarenze papacitos with their child-ones
riding on the high shoulders of hope
carry themselves gingerly through
the pot-holed market streets
ringing with the whored invitation
of border town discotheque balladry
moanin' accordion song visions after
curling up in the doorsteps
from the drizzle and splash
but someday we're gonna ride
out've this desmadre
in a dingo-balled taxi
with the clock punched for the ocean
'til we're dancing to the laughter of the waves
with our tanned bodies wet
and shimmering like mariachi brass

ah-hoo-ah!

## Joaquina

melancholy memory
it's not so strange you should appear
on a night like this
when the sky so dark outside
rumbles with anticipation
as raindrops fall
and the ground begins to hiss

blooming dandelion in spring
uncurling from a cocoon innocence
with eyes looking deep into mine
in the cobweb murmurs of our youth
our hearts were in full bloom
and together we swung back and forth
from the sticky thread of time
beautiful butterfly
where did you fly off to?

I feel the hot breath of desire
forming words into whispers
I respond in black ink silence
while loneliness stands and applauds
and patience like a pigeon cooing on the parapet
cuddles time in its breast
waiting for my napkin poems
and midnight prayers
to wipe away the hurt
and calm my fears

butterfly you'll land again someday
and if I may
I'll climb upon your wings
and together we'll fly off into the dawn
and like the flowers that we sowed
be reborn once more in spring

## Lavender

near
   the old
      faded
turquoise doors

where
   I would
      wait
for you

the
   purple plum
      trees
are in bloom

bridesmaids
   in flowing
      gowns
blushing gleefully

and
   dressed
      in your
favorite color

# A Cowboy Poem for Luci

I wound up
on the wet path
wondering where
you got lost
aphroditic warrior
with mascara and tears
streaming down your cheeks

I came off the hot trail
smelling of saddle leather and dust
and found you looking
like a painted desert blooming
in the crystal glimmer
city-cowboy night

each of our pasts
lingered strong as the taste
of raw whiskey
ah, but our background jitters
soon fell behind
the caressing tune
of a steel guitar

the hot bronc night
spun and bucked
'til I lay bonedry and breathless
watching the sun come up
while your cactus heart
pricked my senses

later on I bled
brewing for your love
under the stars
as I listened to
the lonesome tales
of the yodeling wind

maybe your backyard
picture-window fantasies
of owning a house
overlooking Manhattan Bay

were too noble for my childhood stories
of antique iron and broken clay

may you always keep
a flush card hand
and may you never
stray too far
from a homebound trail

# Purple Hearts

Los Angeles stunk bad
and I could hardly keep
from crying through
bus stop terminal decay

revealing the bones and guts
of a city born
of an american dream
I never knew

where a homeless war vet
stood in the stench
of urine and smog
pleading for loose change

    "so I can eat sir"

reaching out with arms
bombarded by needle tracks
in the shape of tiny
purple hearts

# Daddy's Old Trucks

at night we
would sit with
our father

at the kitchen
table where he
would draw

antique cars and
trucks for me
and my brothers

daddy what does
a '32 Chevy
look like

what about a '34 Ford
daddy now draw
a Model T

and we would ask
him to draw
old trucks

like the one that
our teachers mocked
him for driving

and some of the kids
were reluctant to
be our friends

because we didn't
own a new car
or truck

in class I
would be made
to stand in the corner

because I drew
too many old
cars

I remember

# Magpie Nest

Jerry, Jerry,
    dreams of you
    these dreams of you

phone conversations
hollow as the aching
    in our breasts

but someday we'll return
to the hops of grains
    in our early years

years under yolk sunrises
    yellow as the beaks
    on the chickens
    that roamed the yard

following winding paths
and stoned minds
    weighing heavy

we've been smoking
gray corral boards
twisted from each new
    sparkling January

and walking on hard crust
paths in Ranchos de Taos

sheep pelts on the dry
blue-green-eyed lamb
curly as your black hair
in the morning

when sweet chirps
from the orchard
    trickled down every
    rusted nail point
    on granma's roof

inside the twisting vigas
    down the peeling
    rose-patterned wallpaper

swinging merrily on
the screen door
'n' back out again
    to meet the
    yawning morning

and I would cry
    would cry

if I could

just thinking of the hot
barefoot paths we took
to the post office
on those 9 a.m. summers

heaving cautious
hot sighs across
blistering wood-planked bridge
with nail heads protruding
big as old pennies

1949    In God We Trust

what else can we trust
if not the dime store crosses
    dangling along the soft
    hollows of our necks

where rosary beads
polished smooth and shiny
as nuns' eyes hidden
'neath hoods of repentance
still hum in midnight
    prayer moans

adios, tiempos pasados, adios

new temptations
bred in the dark
yesterday's journey

ring dull
and I dance

a lone monk
in the crowd

# It is May 14th

It is the 14th of May
already the days for planting
are just about over

winter has followed spring unto this season
with afternoon showers of rain, hail,
and cold weather receding into promises
of warm days that come for short spells
and then disappear behind a cloak
of dark clouds and damp weather

the apricots bloomed early
but March also fell prey to frost
and so this year the tree in the back yard
bears no fruit

it is that way sometimes
it is that way in what we have been told

"one year yes, one year no"

it comes down to that
a simple understanding of life's give and take
and we in our lives move forward simply
accepting and giving
as the earth gives
and rejecting and taking
as the earth takes
because we know nothing else

there is nothing else to know
it comes down to that

"un año si, un año no"

and love too
comes in that similar way
and it remains
it remains in that way when it does
like that

so do not be fearful or impatient
learn how to sway
your life accordingly

you will understand what it means
the sound of a horse neighing
in the moonlight
when your season is come

     love

you will know
you will know

# Woodstove of My Childhood

woodstove of my childhood

where potatoes cut like triangle chips were fried
in manteca de marrano

woodstove of lazy autumn smoke swirling away
to nowhere

woodstove of December
evacuating the cold chill at sunrise

woodstove of celebration and mourning

of post-World War II Korea y Vietnam

woodstove corner that kept vigil over
drunken nodding remembrance

woodstove corner where uncles primos compadres
gathered on visits from Califas

woodstove corner with a warm ear for nostalgia

where Mama Ane stirred the atole and wrung her hands
thumb over thumb praying for her children's children's children

woodstove that witnessed six decades washing its face at the vandeja

that saw western swing dancing in dim lantern flame

that watched Elvis come in from across the llano strumming
a mail-order Stella and singing in Spanish

woodstove
of the feast lamb tied up under the crabapple tree

of early sour cherries ripening above the cornstalk horizon

of neighbors bartering a cup of sugar
in exchange for mitote and conversation

woodstove of rain tenderly pouring into the afternoon
and salt sprinkling onto the patio from the mouth of the porch

woodstove of the nighttime crackling softly

of harmonious harmonica medleys
blowing before bedtime prayer

woodstove facing John F. Kennedy's
picture on the wall

woodstove of Protestant Sundays
ringing without bells

woodstove of dark earth
fat worms and acequias

woodstove of 1960s propaganda
and all the rich hippies knocking poorly at the screen door

woodstove of private crazy laughter

of woodpeckers pecking through rough-hewn
barn timbers only to meet the sky

of rabbits nervously nibbling evening away
in the arroyo

of the water bucket banging and splashing
all the way home

woodstove of the water drop sizzle

of buñuelos and biscochitos and flour on the chin

of chokecherry jam dropping out
from the end of a tortilla

woodstove
that heard Mentorcito's violin bringing in the new year

that saw Tío Eliseo bring in an armload of wood

that heard Tío Antonio coming down the road
whistling a corrido and swinging his cane

woodstove of the blessed noontime
and Grandma Juanita heating up the caldito

woodstove of the sanctified and untamed holy spirit

of the dream awake dreamers
prophesizing in the beginning how the end would come

of creaking trochil gates left open forever

of twisted caved-in gallineros rocking
in weeping April wind

of abandoned orchards waist deep
in desánimo

of teardrops that held back the laughter

of the penitente procession moving through the hills
for the soul of the village

woodstove of the wounded faithful proudly
concealing their scars

woodstove of armpit farts and bedtime giggles

of pitchforks and axes under the bed in case of intruders

of coffee cans filled with everything but coffee

of ten cents for a cream soda at Corrina's

of strawberry Nehis and a bag of chili chips at Medina's

of a handful of bubble gum acá Santos's

woodstove of genius wisdom dressed up as the village idiot

of hand-me-down stories locked away
in the dispensa

of bien loco local heroes cracking homeruns
Saturday afternoons en la cañada

woodstove
of all that and more of all that disappearing

as children played hide 'n' seek in that abandoned goodtime feeling
while stumbling on the footsteps of tradition

woodstove that heard the fall of a people rising in silence

that died of a loneliness without cure
that cured itself in the company

of the so many more lonely

woodstove of my childhood

Para todos los paisas:
el que nace
pa resolanero
dondequiera
hace resolana

## Botes de Diez

nos quitamos los sombreros
en saludo de aquellos
que detienen abiertas
las puertas de la locura

dejando entrar y salir
al según vamos trompezando
por el camino chueco
de la vida negra

negra pero alumbrada
con cariños y apoyos
de familiares amigos
y estranjeros

solamente la mano de Dios podrá separarnos

¿y qué fuera
sin la carría
de los babos'
que nos mueve
como chicotasos a que
síganos con la carrera?

carreras laboriosas
que si bien atendidas
al fin disfrutan su jardín
y acarician corazones
con alegría

como las notas
que soplavan de la musiquita
de Don Silviares
en tiempos antepasados

cuando él andava
por los valles
sur de Colorado
vendiendo chile
en carro de caballo

Y especialmente para Tomás y David

que los miro venir
todo el caminito
rascuaches y doblados
con sacos llenos
de cuentos calientitos

pa' desarrollar
por los pueblitos
en estos tiempos
tan fríos y deslumbrados

aquí ando yo
como culebra jardinera
cuidando la milpita
de memorias

y les dejo
una cosechita
de unas cuantas
palabras enpolvadas

y en la manera
de los fruteros
del barrio de los malditos
me despido diciéndoles

"hasta las
        otras piscas,
                plebe"